# FENWAY IN YOUR POCKET

## The Red Sox Fan's Guide to Fenway Park

Kevin T. Dame

Published by Baseball Direct
Central Falls, RI

Design by Christine Dame Yoshida
Illustrations by Ryoji Yoshida, Kevin Dame, and
Christine Dame Yoshida.

Third Printing
Printed in the United States of America

This book may be ordered directly from the publisher by
sending a check or money order for $6.95 per book plus
$2.00 shipping and handling to:
Baseball Direct, P.O. Box 6463, Central Falls, RI 02863.

This book is not endorsed by the Boston Red Sox or
Fenway Park.

*Acknowledgement: This book is dedicated to the 1986
Red Sox, who sparked my incurable fascination with
baseball.*

# Contents

**Preface**

**Chapter One: Fenway Basics**

Fenway Oath .......................................................... 3

Fenway Park: History 101 .............................. 4

Season Time-Line .............................................. 6

Fenway Fast-Facts................................................ 8

**Chapter Two: Pre-Game Prep**

Selecting a Game............................................... 11

Ordering Tickets................................................. 17

The Hazards of Buying From Scalpers .......... 21

Picking the Best Place to Sit ......................... 22

How to Drive to Fenway ................................. 28

Parking Guide..................................................... 32

Alternatives to Driving..................................... 36

What to Bring ...................................................... 38

What Not to Bring.............................................. 39

How to Woo Your Woman into Letting
   You Go to the Game (For Men Only) ......... 40

How to Leverage Your Position of Power
   With Your Man (For Women Only)............... 42

## Chapter Three: Play Ball!

| | |
|---|---|
| Pre-Game Activities | 47 |
| Getting into the Park | 50 |
| Taking Care of the One You Love —<br>Your Stomach | 51 |
| General Information | 55 |
| Following the Game | 56 |
| Characteristics of Fenway | 57 |
| Famous Spots | 65 |
| Fenway Favorites | 67 |
| Talk Like a Fan | 70 |
| Opposing Managers | 75 |
| Dealing with Umpires | 77 |
| Doing the Fenwave | 79 |
| Special Rules for Dealing with Pitchers | 80 |

## Chapter Four: Post-Game Tips

| | |
|---|---|
| Souvenirs | 83 |
| Bowling/Billiards | 84 |
| Night Clubs/Bars | 84 |
| Shopping | 85 |
| Leaving | 85 |

## Chapter Five: Life Beyond Fenway

Alternatives to the Park:
TV and Radio Coverage ............................... 89

PawSox! ............................................. 90

Following the Sox on the Road...................... 92

## Chapter Six: Fanhood Challenge

Multiple Choice Quiz ...................................... 95

Fenway Puzzle ................................................. 101

Fenway in Your Pocket Survey....................... 103

# Preface

**W**hat makes Boston different? Most people respond, "our crazy drivers," and this is a fine answer, given our reputation for absolute chaos on the roadways. A more accurate answer, however, is "our sports." Contrary to what our less intelligent counterparts in New York believe, Boston is the holy land for the avid sports fan. Nowhere in this country can one find the collection of tradition-steeped sports teams combined with such a faithful population of sports fanatics. Moreover, we Bostonians have something truly special that no other sports fan has— Fenway Park.

This book is about Fenway Park, one of the remaining ball parks from baseball's early years. In an era of fabricated nostalgia, Fenway serves as a reminiscent reminder of the way baseball used to be. A night at Fenway is probably little different than one fifty years ago when Ted Williams was terrorizing opposing American League pitchers.

This book is not about boring history or "who cares" trivia. It is a user's guide to Fenway, written for you the Fenway parishioner, to help you get the most out of your experience at the game. It will also help you leave with a few bucks left in your pocket. Whether it's a helpful tip on where to park your car, or a review of the "Fenway Beer Rules," you'll be coached step by step throughout the entire Fenway experience.

I hope you take this guide with you whenever you venture off to the park. I also urge you to fill out the survey in the back of this book with your own ideas and tips on how to enjoy the Fenway experience, and send it to our PO Box address. Your unique perspective will help us to continually improve this guide and help fans enjoy their experience all the more.

As you join the two–million plus fans who enter Fenway's cozy confines this summer, use this guide to its fullest and you'll be guaranteed a great time.

CHAPTER ONE

# *FENWAY BASICS*

# **Fenway Oath**

*"Fenway Park is a shrine where people come for religious rites."* – Former Red Sox pitcher Bill Lee

Before we begin, every Fenway visitor must learn the basic rule of fanhood — the Fenway oath:

*On my honor, I promise to cheer on my Red Sox, to devour Fenway franks and peanuts, to properly execute the "Fenwave," and to soak in the fresh air, smells, sights, and sounds of Fenway, until I am truly at peace.*

Baseball sages have determined that if someday every fan at Fenway could simultaneously achieve this higher level of consciousness for one game, the "Curse of the Bambino," which has stolen many a championship from our grasp, might finally be lifted.

# Fenway Park: History 101

I n 1911, with baseball in its infancy, Red Sox owner John Taylor purchased land in Boston's Fenway section and built a new ball park for the team. Nicknamed "Fenway Park Grounds," it opened in 1912, replete with the latest in ball park design.

The 1912 version of Fenway possessed a steep embankment in front of the left field wall called Duffy's Cliff. The 10 ft. high cliff was named after Red Sox left fielder Duffy Lewis who was known for his defensive prowess around the hill. The cliff was removed in 1933. As the years progressed, Fenway's seating capacity fluctuated. It now stands at 33,871, although more can be squeezed in through the ingenious concept of "standing room only" sections. Fenway's largest crowd occurred on September 22, 1935, when over 47,000 fans attended a game against the arch-rival Yankees. A paltry crowd of 409 cheered on the Red Sox against the Angels on September 29, 1965 representing Fenway's smallest crowd ever.

While Fenway's character and charm have been maintained over the years, there have been some facelifts — most notably the lights added in 1947, the electronic centerfield scoreboard erected in 1976, and the 600 Club (additional indoor seats) in 1988. The 600 Club altered the strong wind currents which formerly traveled outward from home plate. Many experts, particularly over-the-hill power hitters, suspect that this has reduced the frequency of home runs hit at Fenway.

Home runs have always been a part of Fenway's history, starting in 1912 with a seventh inning blast over the wall by Hugh Bradley. Curiously, in the early years there were very few home runs hit by the Sox at home. In fact, in 1916 the Red Sox hit only one home run at Fenway. Three years later a new, livelier baseball was introduced and the Red Sox, led by Babe Ruth's record 29 home runs, hit 33 out of the park.

# Season Time-Line

**T**he true baseball fan realizes that even though the season officially ends in October, in reality it continues on throughout the winter and spring. Your time away from Fenway during the "off-season" is a time to reflect on the previous season, speculate on possible trades and free-agent acquisitions, and to mentally psyche yourself up for the next season. By March you should be experiencing serious withdrawal pains, and eagerly anticipating opening day at Fenway!

# Fenway Fan's Twelve-Month Planner

**January**
Winter ball in S. America

**February**
Players prep for spring training

**March**
Spring Training Games!

**April**
Opening Day!

**May**
Sox pull out in front!

**June**
College baseball draft

**July**
All-Star Game!

**August**
Listen to Sox games on beach

**September**
Pennant Fever!

**October**
Playoffs and World Series

**November**
Debate trades w/friends

**December**
Winter Mtgs: new players for Xmas!

# Fenway Fast-Facts

**F**or those of you who are trapped in today's fast-paced lifestyle, you need the most important information boiled down to a simple, easy to read format that even a chimpanzee could understand. (For the people who typically read USA Today and only read the blurbs on the bottom left of the front page, these FAST-FACTS are for you!)

---

Fenway Park
4 Yawkey Way, Boston, MA 02215
Ticket office: (617) 267-1700
24-hour touch-tone ticketing: (617) 482-4SOX
www.redsox.com

Home games: 81 games (April to October)
Game times: 1:05 pm (Day), 7:05 pm (Night)
TV Coverage: NESN, WFXT
Radio Coverage: WEEI 850 AM

---

**Additional Fast-Facts:** To order the *2000 Red Sox Media Guide,* send $10 to 4 Yawkey Way, Boston, MA 02215. To order the *Official Red Sox Scorebook Magazine,* send $3 to the same address.

CHAPTER TWO

# PRE-GAME PREP

# Selecting a Game

The art of selecting the perfect game is based upon five important factors. Whether it be for your family, the date you're trying to impress, or a business client, considering these five factors will help make your time at Fenway all the more enjoyable:

1. Weather and time of day
2. Time of season
3. The opponent
4. Pitching match-ups
5. Red Sox promotions.

## Weather

It's most important to be comfortable! The prospects of shivering in the face of cold, gusting winds, squinting through your rain-soaked glasses, or passing out due to 90-degree temperatures can all be eliminated if you dress properly for the  weather and time of day. In April, and again in September, you may need a winter jacket, a sweater, and possibly a hat, gloves, and even thermal underwear. Remember, you'll be sitting outside in one place for three hours. For those of you who think that drinking alcohol will keep you warm (college students, pay attention) — you're wrong! The

11

alcohol slows down your metabolism and opens up the pores in your skin. You could actually get hypothermia!

In the middle of the season, during Boston's warmest weather, shorts and T-shirts suffice during the day, while a wind-breaker is usually a good idea to have with you during night games. Certain areas of the park (especially the bleachers) are exposed to strong sunshine, so during the summer make sure to bring a supply of sunscreen or you may end up as red as the players' socks. Reserved Grandstand seats are mostly shielded from the rain, and during a rain delay you will be protected. However, if you are in an unprotected zone (bleachers), make sure you bring a small umbrella just in case of rain. (See "Picking the Best Place to Sit" on page 22 for more information.) Even when rain is forecasted — a common occurrence in Boston summers — grab a wind breaker and umbrella and head to the ball park. It's still worth going because many games are still played after a short delay. You can get a better idea of the like-lihood of a game being called off by calling the Red Sox at (617) 267–8661, or listening to WEEI 850 AM on the radio for the latest weather information.

## Time of Season

The time of season strongly influences ticket availability, the size of crowds, and the general atmosphere inside the park. The first month of the season
is an exciting time for fans (especially opening
day), but seats are a bit easier to get due to the
colder weather. During the dog days of summer
(late July through August), games are often sold
out, yet many fans lose a little interest and turn their
attention to barbecues, trips to the beach, and
members of the opposite sex. In September,
Fenway can be slower if the team is out of con-
tention, but is buzzing with excitement and filled to
the brim with rabid fans if the Sox are battling for
the divisional crown. Because of Fenway's allure
and charm, its slowest moments are still character-
ized by healthy attendance.

## Opponent

"Who are the Sox playing tonight?"—
a common question asked by fans
considering a game. Games against
arch-rivals (Yankees, Orioles) are more exciting and
sought after than against other teams (Angels,
Twins). In fact, attending a Red Sox - Yankees
game at Fenway Park is one of the most intense
experiences in sports.  Note to Yankee fans:  don't
be wearing those pinstripes in our house!

## Pitching Match-Ups

Predicting a game's starting pitcher can be done a few days before the game. This can be accomplished if you know the team pitching rotation. For example, if the Red Sox starting rotation is (1) Pedro Martinez, (2) Ramon Martinez (his brother), (3) Wakefield, (4) Fassero, and (5) Rose, and Pedro Martinez pitched on a Monday, than you can predict with reasonable certainty that Wakefield will pitch on Wednesday night, two days after Pedro Martinez. Star pitchers are always worth going out of your way to see if you appreciate good pitching. If you want to see lots of hits and runs, your best bet is to pick games with the worst pitchers. While the pitching matchups add to the flavor of the game, most fans generally select a game without concern for the pitchers.

**Reading the Pitching Match-Ups in the Newspaper:**
In the Boston Globe Sports Section (or any major newspaper sports page) look for a section entitled "Today's Probable Pitchers/Latest Line" (usually found below the standings). Quite a bit of information can be found in this section, including the game times. Most games begin at 7:05 p.m. on weeknights, and 1:05 p.m. during the day.

Beginning with the left column, you can identify the teams playing one another (the first is the home team). Next to each team is the name of the pitch-

## TODAY'S PROBABLE PITCHERS

### AMERICAN LEAGUE

| | | | 1998 | | Team | 1998 vs. opp. | | | Last 3 starts | | | |
|---|---|---|---|---|---|---|---|---|---|---|---|---|
| | Time | Line | W-L | ERA | Rec. | W-L | IP | ERA | W-L | IP | ERA | AHWG |
| BOS Martinez (R) | 1:35 | -220 | 8-2 | 3.31 | 10-5 | 0-0 | 0.0 | 0.00 | 2-1 | 17.2 | 6.62 | 14.8 |
| At TB Johnson (R) | | | 2-3 | 5.67 | 6-4 | 0-0 | 0.0 | 0.00 | 0-1 | 11.1 | 8.74 | 15.1 |
| KC Pichardo (R) | 1:05 | -115 | 2-6 | 5.96 | 4-3 | 0-0 | 0.0 | 0.00 | 2-1 | 16.0 | 3.94 | 13.5 |
| At DET Harriger (R) | | | 0-1 | 6.75 | 1-3 | 0-0 | 0.0 | 0.00 | 0-1 | 5.1 | 6.75 | 15.2 |
| TOR Hentgen (R) | 1:35 | -115 | 7-4 | 4.35 | 8-7 | 0-0 | 0.0 | 0.00 | 0-0 | 20.1 | 3.54 | 13.7 |
| At BAL Ponson (R) | | | 1-4 | 5.28 | 1-3 | 0-0 | 0.0 | 0.00 | 1-1 | 18.1 | 2.95 | 11.3 |
| MIN Morgan (R) | 2:05 | -115 | 3-2 | 3.95 | 6-8 | 0-0 | 0.0 | 0.00 | 1-1 | 16.0 | 3.38 | 12.4 |
| At CHI Bere (R) | | | 3-6 | 5.94 | 5-9 | 0-0 | 0.0 | 0.00 | 1-1 | 14.2 | 7.36 | 17.2 |
| OAK Oquist (R) | 4:35 | -145 | 4-3 | 5.13 | 6-8 | 1-0 | 7.2 | 2.35 | 2-0 | 19.0 | 5.68 | 11.8 |
| At SEA Swift (R) | | | 6-4 | 4.54 | 6-7 | 0-0 | 0.0 | 0.00 | 2-1 | 15.1 | 1.17 | 11.2 |
| NY Irabu (R) | 8:05 | -120 | 6-2 | 1.68 | 7-4 | 0-0 | 0.0 | 0.00 | 2-1 | 20.1 | 2.21 | 11.1 |
| At CLE Colon (R) | | | 6-4 | 2.73 | 7-7 | 0-0 | 0.0 | 0.00 | 2-1 | 25.2 | 1.40 | 7.0 |
| TEX Perisho (L) | 8:05 | -140 | 0-1 | 23.14 | 5-3 | 0-0 | 0.0 | 0.00 | 0-1 | 2.1 | 23.14 | 30.9 |
| At ANA Dickson (R) | | | 7-4 | 5.43 | 5-4 | 0-0 | 0.0 | 0.00 | 3-0 | 21.0 | 3.00 | 10.3 |

### NATIONAL LEAGUE

| | | | 1998 | | Team | 1998 vs. opp. | | | Last 3 starts | | | |
|---|---|---|---|---|---|---|---|---|---|---|---|---|
| | Time | Line | W-L | ERA | Rec. | W-L | IP | ERA | W-L | IP | ERA | AHWG |
| ATL Neagle (L) | 1:35 | -170 | 8-4 | 3.18 | 10-5 | 1-0 | 7.0 | 1.29 | 1-2 | 24.0 | 3.75 | 9.0 |
| At MON Hermanson (R) | | | 4-6 | 3.20 | 4-7 | 0-0 | 0.0 | 0.00 | 1-2 | 17.0 | 1.59 | 10.6 |
| FLA Fontenot (R) | 1:40 | -350 | 0-4 | 8.14 | 0-5 | 0-0 | 0.0 | 0.00 | 0-2 | 17.0 | 6.35 | 15.9 |
| At NY Leiter (L) | | | 8-3 | 1.53 | 8-5 | 0-0 | 0.0 | 0.00 | 3-0 | 21.0 | 0.86 | 9.0 |
| PIT Loaiza (R) | 2:05 | -150 | 4-3 | 4.73 | 4-6 | 0-0 | 0.1 | 0.00 | 1-2 | 17.0 | 4.24 | 14.3 |
| At MIL Juden (R) | | | 6-5 | 4.08 | 7-8 | 1-0 | 13.0 | 0.69 | 1-1 | 19.0 | 4.26 | 11.8 |
| ARI Daal (L) | 2:10 | -150 | 3-4 | 2.82 | 5-3 | 0-0 | 2.0 | 0.00 | 2-1 | 23.0 | 2.74 | 10.6 |
| At St.L Acevedo (R) | | | 2-1 | 4.68 | 2-2 | 0-0 | 2.0 | 9.00 | 1-0 | 13.0 | 4.85 | 11.8 |
| PHI Green (R) | 2:20 | -165 | 4-4 | 5.21 | 6-8 | 0-0 | 0.0 | 0.00 | 1-0 | 18.2 | 6.27 | 14.0 |
| At CHI Trachsel(R) | | | 6-3 | 4.04 | 9-5 | 0-0 | 0.0 | 0.00 | 0-2 | 19.2 | 6.41 | 13.7 |
| CIN Harnisch (R) | 2:35 | -130 | 6-2 | 2.78 | 7-8 | 0-0 | 0.0 | 0.00 | 1-1 | 21.0 | 1.71 | 9.4 |
| At HOU Schourek (L) | | | 5-4 | 4.70 | 3-5 | 0-0 | 0.0 | 0.00 | 1-2 | 17.0 | 4.24 | 11.6 |
| LA Park (R) | 3:05 | -110 | 5-4 | 4.63 | 8-7 | 0-0 | 0.0 | 0.00 | 1-1 | 21.0 | 3.43 | 10.7 |
| At COL Jones (L) | | | 1-2 | 5.55 | 3-2 | 0-0 | 0.0 | 0.00 | 0-2 | 17.0 | 7.41 | 16.9 |
| SD Brown (R) | 4:05 | -120 | 7-3 | 2.84 | 10-6 | 1-0 | 9.0 | 0.00 | 2-0 | 20.0 | 4.50 | 14.0 |
| At SF Hershiser (R) | | | 6-4 | 3.27 | 10-5 | 0-0 | 0.0 | 0.00 | 1-1 | 16.1 | 4.96 | 17.6 |

KEY: TEAM REC – Team's record in games started by today's pitcher. AHWG – Average hits and walks allowed per game in last 3 starts.

pitcher is R or L, indicating right or left-hander. The time of the game is shown next, along with the odds for those confident enough to bet on a baseball game. The next two columns show the pitchers' performance up to that point in the season. W-L indicates the pitchers' record (wins and losses), and ERA indicates their earned run averages. (ERA is basically the number of runs the pitcher is yielding on average in a 9-inning game.) The rest of the columns provide information about the team's record when the pitcher starts the game, the pitcher's success (or failure) against the opponent this year, the pitcher's performance in his last three starts, and (for the number-crunching rotisserie starts, and (for the number-crunching rotisserie baseball fans) the average number of hits and walks the pitcher has yielded per 9 innings in his last three starts. The acronym for this statistic – AHWG – is surprisingly similar to the sound a pitcher makes after giving up a home run.

## Red Sox Promotions

The Red Sox offer special promotions throughout the year, targetted at younger fans and their families. (This means complimentary souvenirs!) Visit the Red Sox web page (www.redsox.com) for more details on this year's promotions.

# Ordering Tickets

## Walk-up

Tickets can be purchased at either the Red Sox
Ticket Office, (4 Yawkey Way at Fenway Park,
open Monday through Saturday 9 a.m. – 5 p.m;
and open until 7:05 p.m. before night games), or at
the Red Sox Clubhouse shops, located at Copley,
Place, Boston, MA; Burlington Mall, Burlington MA;
and the Emerald Square Mall, North Attleboro, MA.
These locations do *not* accept phone orders. If you
can get to any of these locations during the day,
you will save yourself the grief of either waiting in
long lines before the game to pick up your tickets,
or anxiously waiting for them to arrive in the mail.
Buying tickets in person also saves you the notorious
$6 "handling charge" for your order.

If you're planning a last-minute trip to Fenway
on the day of the game, you must buy your tickets
at Fenway's ticket office, but only up until game
time. If you can't get there in time, you can still buy
tickets from Gate A (see page 50).

## Tickets By Phone

For ticket availability and to purchase tickets, phone the Red Sox at (617) 267-1700, or phone their **24-hour touch-tone ticket line at (617) 482-4SOX**. Master Card, Discover Card, and Visa are accepted. You will pay a $6 shipping and handling charge for the entire order, and if you are ordering 10 days in advance they will mail the tickets to you. Otherwise, you must pick up your tickets before the game at the Reservations Window next to Gate A (see map on page 35 for gate location).

## Tickets By Mail/Fax

If you want to order by mail, specify the date of game(s), the quantity, and the price. Make your check or money order out to "Boston Red Sox." If you are using Master Card, Discover Card, or Visa, include the exact name printed on your card, the card number, and expiration date. Add $6 for shipping/handling for the entire order and include your return address and daytime phone number. Mail your order to Boston Red Sox Ticket Office, 4 Yawkey Way, Boston, MA 02215–3496. Alternatively, you can fax your ticket request information to the Red Sox at (617) 236-6640.

## Internet Ordering

For those of you who find it easier to buy on-line, you can easily buy your Red Sox tickets at "www.redsox.com".

## Discounted Ticket Program

During the course of a season, Fenway typically offers a variety of special games, such as family games (head of household pays full price, rest of family half price), Youth Group games (fans 15 years of age and younger admitted to bleachers or reserved grandstand for half price), Senior Citizen games (fans 65 and over can purchase bleacher or reserved grandstand tickets for half price), and Red Sox promotions (approximately 4 games, various souvenirs given out to fans).

Call the Red Sox Ticket Office at (617) 267–1700, or visit "www.redsox.com", to find out more about these special games.

## Red Sox Ticket Exchange Policy

If you're in a situation where you can't use your tickets, you're in luck. Unlike Celtics, Bruins, and Patriots tickets, you can exchange Red Sox tickets for future games provided you make the exchange at least 1 week before the game. Exchanges are honored for non-season tickets only. Follow the instructions on the back of the tickets.

## Guided Tours

Tours of Fenway are conducted Monday through Friday, May through September, at the following times: 10 a.m., 11 a.m., 12 p.m., and 1 p.m. There are also tours at 2pm on non-game weekdays. Call Fenway Tour Information at (617) 236–6666.

---

### Early Bird Tip!

For the die-hard fan, tickets for the entire season officially go on sale the first Saturday of December. Expect a long line of fans on Yawkey Way for this traditional rite of passage. You can pass the time in line by extolling the virtues of the Sox's latest free agent acquisition.

---

Finally, if you still have questions regarding tickets, try the *Boston Red Sox Ticket Guide,* a sixteen page reference which the Red Sox provide each season.

# The Hazards of Buying From Scalpers

**A** trained eye can pick them out of the crowd. They almost always have an obnoxious, impatient expression and a snake-like demeanor. No, I'm not referring to Yankee fans. I'm talking about scalpers. It is inadvisable to buy tickets illegally through scalpers because of the following possible pitfalls:

1. The scalper sells you tickets with incorrect date.

2. The scalper sells you a pair of tickets which are in different rows.

3. The scalper sells you lousy tickets in supposed "dream location."

4. The scalper does not allow you to reconsider once you are holding the tickets and he has your money.

Note: It is also **illegal** to re-sell a ticket (even at face-value) once it has been purchased.

# Picking the Best Place to Sit

## Bleachers

$14 and $16 — Perhaps the most jovial section in Fenway, it is mostly populated by young, rowdy fans interested in harassing opposing pitchers in the bull pen. These seats are the farthest from home plate (and thus, farthest from the majority of the action), but fans enjoy the section for its fun-loving atmosphere and panoramic view of Fenway from its far corner. The bleachers are great on warm, summer days, but because there is no shade in this area be sure to bring sunscreen. If rain is a possibility, remember that you will be completely exposed to the elements.

Don't let the term "bleachers" mislead you — all the seats have backs, as do all the seats at Fenway. **Section 34** is unique in that it is the furthest bleacher section over towards center field. The lowest rows of **Sections 40 through 43** allow you to watch the pitchers warm up in the bull pens before and during the game. In general, you'll find that all the seats in the bleachers present a clear, unobstructed view of the field.

There are some drawbacks to sitting in the bleachers. Most seats in the bleachers do not have a clear view of the main scoreboard, as it resides above and behind the section. (Although the auxiliary scoreboards which display balls, strikes, the score, etc. can be seen above the first and third base lines.) Also, you will be isolated from the rest of the park, so if you want to walk around and take in the many angles of Fenway you'll find the bleachers too confining.

## Grandstand

$28/$20 — The majority of the seats at Fenway are in the Reserved Grandstand section. Sections 11-31 are $28, while sections 32 and 33 (left field) and sections 1-10 (right field) are only $20. **Sections 5 through 12,** along right field, can become quite uncomfortable because you'll have to strain your neck to the left to follow the action at home plate and the pitchers mound. After about 6 innings, you'll want to turn your head the other way to the right and stare at random people for a couple of innings. (Schedule an appointment with your chiropractor for the next day after the game if you plan to sit in these sections.) If you're not the type to closely monitor every pitch at the plate, you'll find that these sections offer a great view of the entire park. **Sections 1 through 4** are positioned at a more comfortable angle to see home plate, but you'll be almost as far away from home plate as the bleachers are. **Sections 1 and 2** are no-smoking sections.

**Fenway Park Seating**

Sitting along the left field side is a much better prospect. **Sections 28 through 33** are angled towards the playing field. The ideal sections to sit in on the left side are **Sections 24 and 30,** with their clear view of the entire playing field. **Sections 24 through 27, and 13 through 17** also contain prime seats, as you will be seated between home plate and either first or third base. **Sections 32 and 33** should be singled out as unique areas in which to sit because you will be seated right down the left field line next to the Green Monster (see Chapter 3), and have a good shot at watching fair or foul balls fly by your very eyes. **Sections 32 and 33**, however, are non-smoking and alcohol-free zones. **Sections 20 through 23** will seat you directly behind home plate. Many fans enjoy this

**24**

view of the pitcher/hitter confrontation, but must watch it through a protective net.

If you're concerned about rain, be sure to request **rows UU through 16,** which are protected by Fenway's grandstand facade. Sitting in **rows 14 through 16** (the last 3 rows of the section), however, will place you close to the noisy traffic of fans walking to beer and hot-dog stands. In these last few rows you may also be near the "standing room only" area, which sometimes contains tired and impatient fans — many who are often loud and inebriated.

## Loge/Right Field Box Seats

$40/$27 — Seats in the Loge section ($40) are generally the best available seats for those fans that are not season ticket holders. These present great views of Fenway and are close to the field. **Sections 112 through 148** seat you the closest to the infield. Loge seats become Right Field Box Seats at sections 93, and cover sections 86-93. These seats are only $27.

## Roof Box Seats

$40/$27 — These seats place you high above the action on the left or right field sides of the diamond. Infield roof box seats ($40) consist of sections 1-20, with even sections numbers along the 3rd base side of the diamond, and odd sections along the 1st base side. Right field roof box seats ($27) consist of sections 21-43 (odd numbers only).

## Field Box Seats

These seats are best for the baseball aficionado, but are available only to long-time season ticket holders. However, in the late innings don't be shy about sneaking down to these seats. You'll be awed by how close you have suddenly come to the playing field.

## The 600 Club

These seats are generally reserved by corporations for business entertaining, and are located atop Fenway's original structure, high above home plate. It has been blamed for causing the wind to swirl around inside Fenway instead of traveling outward (as it once did), and reducing Red Sox players' home run totals since its construction.

## Private Suites

Again, these seats are available only to season ticket holders, who enjoy drinks, snacks, and television monitors along with the standard menu of Sox entertainment.

## Standing-Room-Only Seats

$7 — Whenever a game is sold out, the standing-room-only area is made available to the public. This area consists of the corridor behind the Reserved Grandstand section, from home plate to right field. Your legs may get tired after several innings, but every die-hard should try this at least once! The Red Sox typically sell out over 50% of their games, so call the Red Sox Ticket Office beforehand to see if these tickets will be available.

## Alcohol-Free Sections

No alcohol is allowed in Reserved Grandstand **Sections 32 and 33** (first-come, first-serve availability).

## Handicapped Seating and Access

Fenway has special rows for wheelchairs and handicapped entrances and seating access. The Red Sox have recently increased their handicapped seating to several Sections. Call the Red Sox Main Office at (617) 267–8661 for details.

# How to Drive to Fenway

## From the Mass. Pike

On Route 90 East (Mass Pike) take the Prudential Exit in Boston (stay left). Take a sharp right off the exit, and at the Sheraton Boston take a right onto Dalton Street. Turn left onto Boylston at the next.light. At the second set of lights, take a right onto Ipswich Street and follow to Fenway (on the right).

## From Rhode Island

On I-95 North follow the Dedham/Maine/New Hampshire split. Take exit 20A/Route 9 East. Travel on Route 9 East for approximately 7 miles. Pass the Chestnut Reservoir, and at the sign for Kenmore Square on the left, take a left onto Brookline Avenue and follow it to Fenway (on the right).

## From Cape Cod

Travel on Route 3 to the Boston split (stay right) and continue northbound on 93 North to Storrow Drive. Take Storrow to the Fenway/Kenmore Square exit (which is a left exit) and stay left. At the top of the exit ramp, bear right onto Boylston Street, and take a right onto Yawkey Way after two sets of lights. Fenway is on the right.

## From New Hampshire (Nashua, Hudson, Amherst)

Travel on Route 3 South to Route 128 South to Route 2 Boston/ Cambridge. Follow Route 2 to the end and bear right at the lights. Pass through the next set of lights and over the bridge (Fresh Pond Mall is on the left). Take a left around the rotary and bear right at the next rotary (don't go around the second rotary). After three sets of lights, follow signs for Storrow Drive. Take Storrow to the Fenway/Kenmore Square exit (which is a left exit) and stay left. At the top of the exit ramp, bear right onto Boylston. After two sets of lights take a right onto Yawkey Way. Fenway is on the right.

## From Coastal New Hampshire and Maine

Travel on I–95 South to Route 1 South towards Boston. Cross the Mystic Tobin Bridge, pay the toll, and merge onto Route 93. Take the first exit, which is Storrow Drive. Take Storrow to the Fenway/Kenmore Square exit (which is a left exit) and stay left. At the top of the exit ramp, bear right onto Boylston. Take a right onto Yawkey Way after two sets of lights. Fenway is on the right.

## From Central New Hampshire and Vermont

Travel on Route 93 South to Boston. At the lower deck of bridge, bear right and follow signs for Storrow Drive. Take Storrow to the Fenway/ Kenmore Square exit (which is a left exit) and stay left. At the top of the exit ramp, bear right onto Boylston. Take a right onto Yawkey Way after two sets of lights. Fenway is on the right.

## Traffic Tips

There are 5 major paths into Boston:

1. Mass. Pike/Route 90 East
2. Expressway Northbound
3. Route 93 South
4. Tobin Bridge
5. Sumner Tunnel

All of these routes are filled with traffic due to the large number of commuters leaving and entering the city, as well as the poor highway design. When afternoon traffic combines with game traffic, congestion can become even worse. The lower deck of the Central Artery, the Sumner Tunnel, the Tobin Bridge, and Storrow Drive are usually jammed with traffic both from commuters passing through the area and the Fenway crowd. **Avoid the Central Artery if at all possible.** On day games, the Tobin Bridge, the lower deck, and the expressway are not so bad because the commuters are gone. Also,

Route 9 (Boylston Ave.) can be a good option but is still slow because there are too many traffic lights. The Mass. Pike is the least congested and easiest route from the highway.

Your best bet is to listen to WBZ 1030 AM, which provides traffic updates every 10 minutes on the :03 minute. Before heading to the game, check the updates for major traffic jams or accidents.

Of these routes, the Mass Pike is by far the least likely to become congested. You will have to pay tolls, but it's worth the aggravation you'll spare yourself.

If you hate driving in traffic, you may want to consider taking the rapid transit line from Braintree, or parking farther away from Fenway and walking.

# **Parking Guide**

**P**arking near Fenway can be irritating, time consuming, and a ripoff if you don't know what you're doing. For the educated fan, however, parking near Fenway can be a simple exercise.

### **Rating Key**

★★★★ Fenway connoisseur's choice

★★★ Seasoned Boston sports fan's pick

★★ Only under extreme time duress

★ Watch out for the man with the slim-jim!

## **1. Masco Lot ★★★**

Corner of Brookline and Yawkey. For $10 your car will be parked outside without being boxed in. You will see a sign "Red Sox Ticket Office across street," and the lot is located to the left of this sign, next to Boston Beer Works. This lot is often full.

## **2. Landsdowne Garage ★★★**

Landsdowne Street across from park. The cost is $10, with most cars parked indoors, and none boxed in. This seems like a good deal.

### 3. VIP Parking ★★★

Corner of Yawkey and Van Ness (and other adjacent lots). The cost is $15, almost all the cars are unblocked, and some are even parked inside a garage. This lot is staffed by several red-shirted, professional attendants. They will keep your keys during the game.

### 4. Leahy Mobil ★

Corner of Boylston and Yawkey. For $20 your car will be parked with a chance of being boxed in.

### 5. LAZ Parking ★★

(Pronounced "lazy") Corner of Yawkey and Van Ness. For $15 your car is parked without being boxed in.

### 6. LAZ Parking ★★

Corner of Ipswich and Van Ness. For $15, your car will be parked without being boxed in. A lazy choice.

### 7. Texaco Parking ★

Corner of Boylston and Ipswich. You pay $20 to have your car boxed in while an attendant walks around with a slim jim for "emergencies."

## 8–9. Best Bets

### 8. Parking Away From the Park ★★★★

If you are willing to park farther away and walk or take the subway to the park, you will save yourself a great deal of grief from the nightly traffic jam around Fenway after the game. If you can, park on Brookline Ave. or Beacon St. in the metered spots. This will leave you with an enjoyable 5–10 minute walk to the park.

### 9. The Prudential Center Garage ★★★★

The best bet is to park at the **Prudential Center Garage,** located on Boylston Street between Dartmouth and Exeter, and walk to Fenway. Get there from the Mass. Pike by taking the Prudential Center/Copley exit. You'll pay only $5 for parking if you present your ticket stub after the game. Your car will be parked indoors, unblocked, and you keep the keys. What's even better is that you can stay parked there from 5 p.m. to 1 am. To leave the lot after the game, simply turn off Boylston, take a left on Newbury, and you'll be back on the Mass. Pike in two blocks.

# Fenway Fan's Parking Guide

Numbers correspond to parking guide on pages 32–34.
Letters correspond to Fenway Park gate entrances.

# Alternatives to Driving

## Walking to the Game

Most walking routes to Fenway through the city are enjoyable. If you have some extra time before the game, take a stroll through the Back Bay down Commonwealth Avenue or Newbury Street, towards Fenway. After crossing Mass. Ave, continue down Commonwealth or Beacon. You should avoid walking through the Back Bay Fens, a park located near Fenway (see map on page 31). This area may seem inviting, but it is not safe to walk through, especially at night. When you reach Kenmore (via Commonwealth or Beacon), take a left onto Brookline.

## Public Transportation

Taking the MBTA (affectionately called "the T") is a simple and cheap way of getting to and from Fenway if you don't want to walk or drive. Subways on the Green Line tend to get crowded before and after the game, so don't expect to sit. Fenway is located off the Green Line at the Kenmore Square stop. This puts you on Commonwealth Avenue. Take a left on Brookline and walk to Fenway. When you leave Fenway simply follow the directions in reverse. The last train to Braintree leaves Boston at 12:30 am. For more information about other commuter rail routes, call the MBTA at (617) 374–1234.

Map courtesy of the MBTA ©

# What to Bring

**O**bserve the weather conditions, dress appropriately, and bring the necessary extras such as a wind-breaker for windy, colder weather, an umbrella in case of rain, and sunscreen on sunny days. Sporting white and red garments will reinforce your Red Sox loyalty, as will wearing a Red Sox hat or T-shirt. Since you will most likely be sitting in the "common-man" areas, don't wear expensive, silk garments, because spilled bear or mustard are facts of life at any ball park. Small children and infants should be wrapped in swaddling Red-Sox colors. Sun-glasses (and regular glasses) are a plus, as are opera glasses or binoculars. You are allowed to bring a camera, so if it's convenient bring it and capture Fenway's colorful charm. Be careful about bringing too many things, however, as there is very little room in front of and under your seat. One last thing...make sure to bring this guide!

# What Not to Bring

First, avoid wearing hats and/or paraphernalia from other baseball teams (especially the Yankees). Harmless as it may seem, you risk being harassed by Red Sox fans in your section. Also, there are several items which Red Sox security will not allow you to enter with: beach balls, inflatable dolls (yes, they have had problems with them in the bleachers), alcoholic beverages, beverages in glass bottles, and aluminum cans. If you're bringing a lunch, Fenway security may search your bags and ask you to leave cans and bottles behind.

# How to Woo Your Woman into Letting You Go to the Game (For Men Only)

**M**en, you all know how hard it can be to unshackle that ball and chain from your leg and get out to the Park. But that's the price you pay for love! Whether it's your girlfriend, fiancée, or wife, try these proven techniques which will produce measurable results for you:

**PLAN A:** Walk in the house/apartment and pretend that she's already agreed to go to the game. Stride in confidently, and while hurriedly changing your clothes, remark, "OK, honey, are you almost ready to go to the park?" This technique works most effectively if she has a poor memory.

**PLAN B:** If Plan A fails, imply that some commitment exists, one which would be difficult to break. "But honey, the Johnsons have already planned to go with us." Or, "Dear, I already bought the tickets over the phone!"

**PLAN C:** If Plans A and B have failed, it's time to really put on the charm. Try sweet cooing noises in her ear, followed by an innocent, "Please, can't we go to the game tonight?" in a baby-like quiver.

**PLAN D:** If Plan C doesn't work, you're going to have to make some sacrifices. Promise to take out the garbage, iron the shirts, wash the dishes, or any other chores that need to be done when you return from the game. (Don't worry, when you get back from the game, simply collapse in bed and feign a heavy sleep.)

**PLAN E:** If she won't go for Plan D, try relating to her a poignant childhood story of when your dad took you to your first game at Fenway, and allow your voice to "choke up" a bit. (Attempting this technique while dicing onions is most effective.)

**PLAN F:** If she complains that the game is just too boring, assault her with a flurry of rebuttals, such as citing the great weather, or the current Sox winning streak. Entice her with a delicious "dinner out" before the game (Wink wink: it will be those great sausages outside Fenway!). You can also try, "Honey, we don't have to stay for the whole game" (cross fingers behind back). If all else fails, try the line, "Don't you enjoy my company anymore?" with your head cocked at a pitiful angle with sad puppy eyes.

**PLAN G:** If nothing has worked up to now, you're in trouble. Drop to your knees, grab her legs and feet, and start begging. Don't let go until she gives in.

# How to Leverage Your Position of Power With Your Man (For Women Only)

So, your man is always harassing you about letting him go to sporting events. But shackling him in the house isn't the answer. You must use a two-pronged strategy:

1. Go to a game with him. If you're already a fan, treat yourself to a night out in the fresh air and enjoy just being together. If you're not yet a fan, go anyway! You will gradually learn to love baseball, and actually enjoy the outings. How do you become a baseball fan? Well, by reading this book cover to cover you'll know more about Fenway than he does. Start reading the sports section of the newspaper (in private, of course!), and various sports magazines such as *Sports Illustrated*. Also, watch the sports segment of the evening news. If you're puttering around the house, listen to the Sox on the radio.

2. And now the more critical part: pretend you are not really that big of a sports fan, but are joining him because you love him so much! This allows you to leverage your power position — you are in the driver's seat now! The way to do this is through the magic of...

## ...THE POINT SYSTEM!!

Even if you are a fan, you can still pretend you're not up for it (headache, long day at work, weather, etc.). Every time you "do him a favor" by going to the game, assign a certain number of points to this favor (the two of you will agree on this number each time), and you'll find that it can become quite large when the Sox are playing the Yankees, or the weather outside is gorgeous. Now that you've agreed on the value of the favor, get it in writing. Create a table of favors, with various point values for each favor. Whoever has fewer points owes the other favors.

If the game is worth 3 points, for example, and he's in the red for three games (total of 9 points owed), think of all the great things he has to do for

you! With his passion for sports, you'll probably always be on the receiving end. And he won't resent you for these favors because, after all, it is you who is allowing him to go to the game!

## Sample Point Sheet

Back rub .......................2 points
Paint toe nails.................2 points
Do dishes .......................1 point
Treat dinner out.............3 points
Flowers all week.............5 points
Girls night out ................4 points

CHAPTER THREE

# *PLAY BALL!*

# Pre-Game Activities

**O**n radio station WEEI 850 AM, there is a pre-game show 30 minutes before the game, with players and the Red Sox manager and general manager interviewed nightly. Tailgate barbecuing is not an option because you will most likely be parked in tightly with other cars and won't have room for a barbecue (save this for a Patriots game!). If you want to have a snack, a drink, or a meal before the game, here are some suggestions:

## Eat in the Park

The absolute best pre-game activity is getting into the park early, munching on some Fenway Franks, and taking in batting practice. The food inside the park is decent, and reasonably priced. Besides, the true baseball fan eats ball park food, not fancy restaurant cuisine!

## Boston Beer Works

At the corner of Brookline and Yawkey, this restaurant/bar offers appetizers such as nachos and half-back ribs, full meals ranging from beer-basted burgers to various pasta dishes, and several kinds of house brews. You can watch the game or other sporting events on monitors there.

## Cask 'n Flagon

Located at the corner of Landsdowne and Brookline. Similar to Boston Beer Works, this establishment has been a Fenway pre-game watering hole for years. They offer a full compliment of appetizers, meals, and adult beverages, along with a big-screen TV, and various games (video, basketball, etc.). This place is usually mobbed with pre-game partiers.

## Pizzeria Uno

Located at the Corner of Beacon Street and Brookline (645 Beacon St.), this Pizza Restaurant offers Chicago-style deep-dish pizzas and the usual standard appetizers and desserts. This restaurant becomes jam-packed before games, so you should get there several hours before the game to beat the crowd.

## Cornwall's Bar/Pub

Located below ground level between the Army/Navy Store and Dunkin' Donuts at 510 Commonwealth Avenue (across from the Kenmore subway stop), this small but homey pub possesses a "Cheers-like" atmosphere. Season ticket holders often arrive before the game for beers, burgers, Cajun chicken, and the fish of the day.

## Linwood Grill

Another great option is to check out the Linwood Grill, located at 81 Kilmarnock (see map on page 35). This restaurant offers great southwest barbeque including ribs, pulled pork, and fixin's like mashed potatoes and cornbread. They also offer a variety of appetizers and entrees such as sea bass and salmon. The Linwood has an adjoining club that features bands on Thursday, Friday, and Saturday nights (starting at 10pm).

## Outdoor Food Vendors

You will find 6-7 sausage vendors along Landsdowne Street. These sausages (priced at $4) are smothered in peppers and onions on a roll. You can also find steak or Cajun chicken sandwiches for $5.

# Getting Into the Park

*Whew, I thought we would have to call in the fire department, my team's so hot." – Casey Stengel, after his NY Mets snapped a 17-game losing streak.*

You can enter the park up to an hour and a half before game time. This is your chance to see the players take batting practice and shag fly balls in the outfield. Try to go early, or, at least, to be on time so that you can watch the players take the field, and sing the National Anthem. Don't be like Los Angeles Dodger fans, who are known for arriving late and leaving early!

Entering Fenway can be a frustrating experience — many fans wander around the entire ball park trying to find the right entrance. **Gate A** is the main gate, and the place to pick up prepaid tickets. For the bleachers, enter through **Gate C** (located on Landsdowne St.). If you're sitting in right field, enter through **Gate B** (Ipswich Street), left field through **Gate E** (Brookline and Landsdowne), and anywhere in between the infield section through **Gate A** (Yawkey Way). **Gate D** is reserved for private suites and roof boxes. (See map on page 35 for gate locations.)

# Taking Care of the One You Love — Your Stomach

**F**ind your seat first — then get your food. There is nothing worse than staggering through crowded Sections of the park, arms full of teetering sodas and food, with your ticket in your mouth, trying to find your row ("excuse me, pardon me..."). It is also unpleasant for the other people you are disturbing.

There are roughly 20 concession stands throughout Fenway (5 located in the bleachers, 7 in right field, 2 in left field, and 2 behind home plate). There are several more on the upper and roof levels. Most stands offer hot dogs, sausage, popcorn, beer and soda. The exception is pizza, for which there are two stands in the entire park. These stands, called "Pizza Plus," sell cheese and pepperoni pizza by the slice or in whole form. If you want pizza, head directly behind **Section 20** (behind home plate), or in the bleachers, and you will find "Pizza Plus" (with its traditional long line), and "Beer Express" next door.

If you're lazy and decide to wait for a vendor to come by with food, you may be waiting a long time for your dinner. Vendors only distribute hot dogs, soda, peanuts, and ice cream sports bars. You'll have to get up and seek out your beer, pizza, and other snacks.

# Fenway Fan's Food Guide

Kids Dog

Fenway Frank

Ft. Long Dog

Polish Sausage

Hamburger

Cheeseburger

Chicken Sandwich

Italian Sausage with peppers & onions

Steak & Cheese

Cheese Pizza

Pepperoni Pizza

Clam Chowder

Kids Meal ( Dog, 12oz. Souvenir Soda, 5oz. Goldfish

Kids Soda 12oz. (Coke, Diet Coke, Sprite)

Reg. Soda 21oz.

Souv. Soda 32oz.

Lemonade 28oz.

Candy

Cotton Candy

Sm. Cracker Jacks (1.25oz.)

Lg. Cracker Jacks (8oz.)

Sm. French Fries

Lg. French Fries

Sm. Nuts 4oz.

Lg. Nuts 7oz.

Sm. Popcorn

Lg. Popcorn

Sm. Nacho

Lg. Nacho

Cookies (Pepperidge Farm Milano/ Nantuckets)

Pretzel 5oz.

Potato Chips 1oz.

Frutopia 12oz. can

Bottled water 16.oz (Poland Springs)

Coffee 10oz.

Hot Chocolate

Powerade (20 oz. bottle)

## Fenway Fan's Food Guide (continued)

Coke, Diet Coke, Sprite
(20 oz. bottle)

Hot/Iced Cappuccino
16 oz.

Ice Cream
Sports Bar

Soft Serve
Cone/Cup

Soft Serve
Souv. Helmet

Luigi's ice Popup
8oz.

Draft Beer 12oz.

Prem. Draft 12oz.

Non-alcoholic Beer
(O'Douls, Cutter,
Sharps 12oz. can)

Combo Meal (Ital.
Sausage & 20oz.
bottled soda)

## Fenway Beer Rules

If you like to drink a few beers during a ball game, you should become familiar with "the beer rules." Study them, commit them to memory, for they shall govern your consumption at Fenway.

**Rule 1:** Thou Shalt buy only two beers at a time.

**Rule 2:** Thou Shalt not buy a beer without identification.

**Rule 3:** Thou Shalt leave your seat to seek out beer.

**Rule 4:** Thou Shalt not buy beer after the 7th inning.

**Rule 5:** Thou Shalt not drink beer in Sections 32 and 33.

**Rule 6:** Thou Shalt not consume too much beer and be removed by security.

# General Information

**Telephones**

Four phones are located under Reserved Grandstand **sections 32/33, sections 21/22, sections 23/24, and section 6.** In addition you will find a phone in the bleachers under **sections 36/37**.

**Men's/Ladies' rooms**

In the Reserved Grandstand area, men's rooms are located in left field, between home and 1st base, and in right field. Ladies' rooms can be found in left field, between home and third base, behind home plate, and in right field. The bleachers contain 1 men's and 1 ladies' room.

**Customer Service Booths**

These booths are located behind home plate and under the bleachers.

**Souvenir Stands**

The Landsdowne Shop, located behind **Section 30** in the Reserved Grandstand, has authentic and replica souvenirs. There are also smaller souvenir stands scattered throughout the park.

**First Aid**

Located under **section 13** in concession area.

**Lost and Found**

If you lose anything report it immediately at the information booth or call (617) 267-9440.

# Following the Game

**D**uring the course of the game you will discover several areas of the park which provide you with information on player statistics, the score of the game, the score of other games in progress, and the current number of strikes, balls, and outs.

There are two small auxiliary scoreboards along the left and right field Grandstand facades. The illustration below shows these scoreboards during a game between NY and Boston. The scoreboards show runs (R), hits (H), errors (E), the current inning (Inn), the current hitter's number (AB), balls (B), strikes (S), and outs (O).

The main scoreboard, located deep in center field behind the bleacher sections, shows player statistics, and sometimes replays spectacular catches or home runs. Announcements, along with the Bickford's Baseball Quiz, and the "Guess the Attendance" game, are shown on this main scoreboard. Most fans follow the game by the traditional, manually operated scoreboard located in left field, (see Left Field Scoreboard on page 59).

# Characteristics of Fenway

## Dimensions

While every ball park in baseball possesses its own unique dimensions, Fenway has by far the most interesting geometry. Home run hitters drool over the short distance from home plate down the left field line to the Green Monster, which reads a meager 315 feet. Fenway's dimensions are 302 feet to the right field foul pole, 380 feet down the right field line, a long 420 feet to deep center, 379 feet to the right of the Green monster in Left-Center Field, and an eye-opening 315 feet down the left field line to the foul pole.

The distance from home plate to the left field wall is controversial. Although "315 ft" is painted on the wall, almost everyone familiar with Fenway and the Red Sox disbelieves this number. In 1975 the Boston Globe used aerial photography to measure it at 304.779 feet. The Red Sox refuse to allow anyone to measure it, adding to the mystery.

The crowd is close to the field at Fenway, creating an intimacy not found in other ball parks, as well as the smallest foul territory in the league. Fenway's nooks and crannies in left, center, and right, the triangular nature of the bleachers, and its majestic left field wall (called the Green Monster) make it totally unique to other sporting arenas.

## The Green Monster

(Also known as "The Wall.") Fenway's most famous attraction, the Green Monster, is known for its close proximity to home plate, its height, and its built-in scoreboard. Its presence can be a double-edged sword for hitters and pitchers alike. Routine fly balls become home runs if the wind is blowing out (watch the flag in center field for gusts of wind). Its towering height of 37 feet trans-forms high, lazy fly balls into cheap extra-base hits as the ball caroms  off its surface on the way down. The Wall, however, can cut down heat-seeking, missile-like home run shots that are hit too low, turning them into doubles or even singles. Balls hit off the wall are called "wall-balls." Sometimes, balls are hit right at the scoreboard and bounce off at odd, unpredictable angles. This can create a nightmarish experience for the left fielder.

The Green Monster did not always look the way it does today. In 1947, The Wall was mostly covered with picture ads. The net above The Wall was installed in 1936 to protect windows on Landsdowne St. from home run balls. Before it was resurfaced with hard plastic in 1976, The Wall con-sisted of wooden railroad ties, covered with tin. Balls hit off the tin portion of The Wall would drop straight to the ground with a thud. The Green

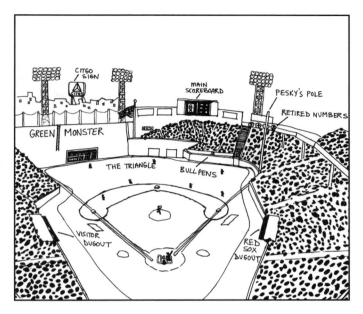

Monster possesses the league's only "in-play" ladder, which starts 13-1/2 feet above the ground and rises along the left corner of The Wall. It is used by groundskeepers to retrieve balls hit into the net during batting practice and during the game.

## Left Field Scoreboard

You will find the grand-daddy of all scoreboards in left field, located on the Green Monster. It is one of only two original manually-operated scoreboards in baseball. (Wrigley Field in Chicago has the other.) This scoreboard shows inning-by-inning totals of each team's runs, and keeps totals of hits,

| | A M E R I C A N | | L E A G U E | | | |
|---|---|---|---|---|---|---|

| P | | 1 2 3 4 5 6 7 8 9 10 | R H E | P | IN R | P | IN R |
|---|---|---|---|---|---|---|---|
| 37 | K.C. | 0 0 0 3 0 0 | 3 5 0 | 36 NY | 2 | 36 NY | 2 |
| 49 | BOSTON | 2 0 1 0 0 | 3 5 0 | 35 CLEV | 3 1 | 35 CLEV | 3 1 |
| | | | | 46 BALT | 1 | 46 BALT | 1 |
| AT BAT | BALL STRIKE OUT (H) | (E) | | 37 TOR | 2 1 | 37 TOR | 2 1 |
| 24 | ●●● ●● ●● ● | ● | | 49 DET | | 49 DET | |
| | | | | 40 CHI | | 40 CHI | |

runs, and errors. Watch for the numbers to change when a run is scored. Each number is 16" x 16", weighs 3 lbs., and is changed manually by Fenway personnel. If you look closely, you will see a faint outline of a door leading behind the wall. Before the game Fenway personnel can be seen walking in and out through this door.

The scoreboard's charm comes in part from the traditional green and red bulb lights which indicate balls, strikes, and outs (red for strikes and outs, and green for balls). The "out of town" portion apprises you of the scores of all games being played that day in the American League. You may wonder what the two-digit number next to each team means. It represents the uniform number of the pitcher currently in the game for each team. Finally, the initials of the late Red Sox owners, Thomas A. Yawkey (TAY) and Jean R. Yawkey (JRY) appear in Morse code in two vertical stripes.

## CITGO Sign

Built in 1965 atop a building on 660 Beacon St. in neighboring Kenmore Square, this Fenway mainstay looms behind the Green Monster.

## Jimmy Fund Sign

This sign is located in right field above the Grandstand. The Jimmy Fund has raised millions of dollars for the Dana Farber Cancer Institute in its fight against cancer in children.

## Right Field

Fenway's right field is considered to be one of the most problematic to field in baseball, due to the close proximity of the bull pens to home plate and the odd angles the fielder must deal with if a ball is hit in the corner. This area is formed by the low railing and wall which curve out sharply from the pole into deep right field. Many cheap home runs have occurred as weak 302-foot pop-ups sail just past the foul pole into the stands.

## Pesky's Pole

The right field foul pole was nicknamed "Pesky's Pole" by a sports-writer after former Red Sox player Johnny Pesky hit the pole for a game-winning home run.

## Visitor and Home Bull Pens

In 1940, the Red Sox, in part to help Ted Williams hit home runs, added the bull pens in right field. This addition, nicknamed "Williamsburg," reduced the distance from home plate by 23 feet. These "pens" are the place where the bull pen pitchers eat sunflower seeds, spit tobacco, play pranks on one another, warm-up, and watch the game until the bull pen phone rings. (Yes, the manager actually picks up a phone and calls the bull pen when he

wants a pitcher to begin warming up.) Pitchers warming up in the pen quickly become subjected  to crowd praise or abuse. When called upon, they enter the playing field through the bull pen doors, and trot across the outfield to the pitcher's mound.

## Retired Numbers

Located on the green facade atop Fenway's right field Grandstand, you will see five red numbers on white, circular back-grounds. Four of the five numbers (1, 4, 8. and 9) are the num-  bers of the four Red Sox players whose numbers have been retired due to the following criteria: the players were inducted into the Baseball Hall of

Fame, played at least 10 years with the Red Sox, and ended their careers with the Red Sox. The numbers read 9 for Ted Williams, 4 for Joe Cronin, 1 for Bobby Doerr, and 8 for Carl Yastrzemski. The fifth number (42) was added to honor Jackie Robinson, a tribute to his breaking baseball's color barrier.

The Red Sox recently re-ordered the retired numbers from their original configuration of 9, 4, 1 and 8. This earlier configuration had to come to symbolize 82 years of futility in attaining a World Championship, often termed "The Curse of the Bambino," in reference to the Red Sox sale of Babe "the bambino" Ruth to the Yankees. The numbers, reading 9-4-1-8, match with September 4, 1918, the eve of the 1918 World Series. Babe Ruth would pitch the next day, win the first game of the series 1–0, and lead the Red Sox to their last World Series victory. A year later Red Sox owner Harry Frazee, financially strapped with the team and his theater business, would strike up a deal in which he would sell Babe Ruth to the Yankees for $100,000 in cash and a $300,000 loan in the form of a mortgage on Fenway Park. Since then, the Yankees have won 24 World Championships, while the Red Sox have come up empty.

During the 2000 season, The Red Sox will retire number 27, honoring Carlton Fisk, one of the greatest catchers in baseball history.

## The 600 Club

This structure, which resides high above home plate, was added to Fenway in 1988, and consists of luxury boxes for the corporate crowd. Many have speculated that it has altered wind currents which originally traveled across the field and over the Green Monster. It has been blamed for a reduction in home runs hit by the Red Sox since the addition was made. Students at MIT have conducted numerous studies which seem to support this theory, and once planned to propose, design, and test a wind-altering device which would redirect wind back over the wall.

# Famous Spots

**B**esides being a baseball heaven, Fenway also serves as a virtual museum of Red Sox history. Here are a few slices of Fenway's past.

## Foul Pole in Left Field

Carlton Fisk's famous 12th inning home run on October 22, 1975 in the World Series against Cincinnati stands as one of baseball's finest moments. Fisk's hooking drive bounced off the foul pole as he ran down the first base line, contorting his body, willing the ball to stay fair. At 12:33 a.m., all of New England rejoiced in the knowledge that the Red Sox had forced a 7th and deciding game, and an opportunity for their first World Series victory since 1918.

## Right Field in Front of Bull Pens

Dwight Evans' famous catch in right field (in the same game) robbed the Reds' Joe Morgan of extra bases or even a home run, which would have lost the game and the Series for the Red Sox. Evans caught the ball on the run over his shoulder, turned, and fired to first base, picking off the runner for an inning-ending, game-saving double play.

## Bleachers

Only six balls have ever been hit out of the park to the right of the flag pole in center field. These hitters were: Hank Greenberg and Jimmy Foxx in 1937, Bill Skowrun in 1957, Carl Yastrzemski in 1970, and Bobby Mitchell and Jim Rice in 1976.

## Pitcher's Mound

In 1986, up-and-coming pitcher Roger Clemens, in the fourth game of his first full season with the Red Sox, shocked the baseball world by striking out a record 20 Seattle Mariners, breaking the record of 19 shared by Steve Carlton, Nolan Ryan, and Tom Seaver. The Sox won the game 4–1 and went on to win the American League Pennant.

## Home Plate

During the final home game of the 1960 season, Red Sox great Ted Williams stepped to the plate in the 8th inning for the last time in his long career. The "Splendid Splinter" drove the last pitch he saw into the right field bull pen, and the crowd paid tribute with a thundering ovation as he rounded the bases one last time.

# Fenway Favorites

## Fenway Sights

- Walking from the far corner of left field (next to the Green Monster) to the far corner of right field (next to Pesky's pole), along the pathway in the lower Grandstand area. When you start out, take a good look at the Green Monster and its intimidating presence. Take in the various vantage points of the game as you work your way to right field.

- Participating in the "Fenwave," which usually starts in the bleachers, and almost always travels clockwise through the bleachers, into right field, and on through to left field.

- Watching the manager and the umpire arguing, escalating to the point where both are less than an inch apart, spraying saliva on each others faces, and always yelling at the same time.

- Watching the cleaning crew primp and preen the infield dirt and mound between the 5th and 6th innings.

- Watching beach balls ricochet around the bleachers, or even better, being in the bleachers and striking one of the balls.

- "Wall-ball," a game played frequently at Fenway, where the batter hits the ball at the Green Monster. The ball ricochets off the wall or scoreboard at weird, unpredictable angles, causing the unfamiliar, panic-stricken, visiting outfielder to scramble after the elusive ball.

- Watching the red and green lights on the Green Monster scoreboard whenever a strike, ball, or out is recorded.

- The grounds crew, under the tyrannical, militant leadership of Joe Mooney, covering the field during a rain delay.

- Witnessing the crowd's and players' reaction to a squirrel or a rat racing across the outfield.

- Watching a run changed manually on the left field scoreboard, and watching a score change on the "out-of-town" scoreboard during a pennant race as a rival team is embroiled in a close game in the late innings.

# Fenway Sounds and Smells

- The home plate umpire howling or grunting a called third strike on a bewildered batter.

- The crescendo of the crowd cheering as a well struck ball rises majestically over the Green Monster and into the night for a home run.

- The National Anthem, and "Take Me Out to the Ball game," sung during the 7th inning stretch.

- The combination of mustard, hotdogs, fresh air, cigar smoke, bubble gum, and roasted peanuts: a unique scent only found in baseball parks.

- The smell of the leather of a baseball glove that you've brought to track down foul balls.

- The smell of sizzling sausages outside of Fenway Park at the vendor carts.

# Talk Like a Fan

*"Whenever I decided to release a guy, I always had his room searched first for a gun. You couldn't take any chances with some of those birds." – Casey Stengel*

I f you really want to be part of the "Fenway faithful," you need to master the slang, the delivery, the attitude of a true Red Sox fan. The basic idea is to be wildly biased towards the Sox, wildly opposed to the other team, and fickle with the umpires. Booing should be reserved for members of the other team, and only under extreme conditions is it acceptable to lay your wrath on a Red Sox player. (Extreme condition example: The Red Sox clean-up hitter has not hit a home run in 2 months, is hitting below .200, has stranded 6 runners in the game thus far, and has just struck out with the bases loaded with the Red Sox down by 2 runs.)

## Slang

Mastering Fenway fanhood also involves the use of baseball slang. Mastering the Boston accent can take years of practice, and is almost impossible to imitate properly by the novice. Your correct usage of words and expressions, however, will allow you to feel at home with the established "Fenway Faithful" in your section.

## Sure-fire Expressions

The use of short, colorful expressions is common among Fenway fans. They are used primarily to summarize or observe situations on the field. They are often filled with emotions such as awe, sarcasm, wonder, cynicism, panic, or anger. Here are a few examples:

**When the hitter strikes out:**

- Say to the person sitting next to you, "He whiffed!!" or "He was blown away!"

- Yell at the player as he walks back to the dugout, "See ya!" or "Sit down!" or "Back to the minors!"

**When the opposing pitcher is pitching poorly:**

- Say to the person sitting next to you, "He's being lit up!" or "He's being shelled/ shellacked/ knocked around!"

- Yell to the pitcher after a big hit, "Nice pitch, Stottlemyre!" or "Give him another cookie, Stottlemyre!"

- Also, signal to the bull pen by touching outstretched arm (like manager does when he requests a pitching change).

**When a Red Sox pitcher is wild:**

- Say to the person sitting next to you, "He's all over the place!" or "He's got control problems!" or "He can't find the plate!"

• Yell to the pitcher as the count goes to 3 balls, no strikes, "Throw Strikes!"

**When the opposing pitcher is removed from the game after a poor performance:**

• Yell, "Sayonara!" or "Hit the showers," or "Back to the minors!"

• Sing along with organ, "Nah, Nah, Nah, Nah... Nah, Nah, Nah, Nah.... Hey, Hey, Hey... Goodbye!" (Raise beer while singing.)

Practice these phrases and study the slang guide on the next three pages.

# Guide to Fenway Slang

| Slang | What it Means | Secondary Meaning |
|-------|---------------|-------------------|
| Aspirin tablet | fastball | cure for hangover |
| Baltimore chop | weak hit chopped off front of plate | imitation of Atlanta fans |
| Banjo Hitter | poor contact, makes sick sound | musician at bat |
| Batting practice pitch | weak, easy-to-hit fastball | pitch thrown during practice |
| Beanball | pitch which hits the batter | eatable pitch |
| Boot | fielding error | for illegally-parked car |
| Bridge Master | pitcher who allows too many homeruns | card-game genius |
| Brush back | pitch intentionally thrown close to batter | a useful shower tool |
| Bum | lousy player (used liberally for pitchers) | a person's underside |
| Bush league | lacking class (minor leaguer) | league for ex-presidents |
| Cheese | fastball | eatable mold |
| Chump | bum — used primarily for hitters | cousin of the chimpanzee |
| Comebacker | ball hit back at pitcher | boxer who keeps getting up |
| Cookie | an easy to hit pitch (see BP pitch) | a cute name for significant other |
| Cup of coffee | brief stint in majors with a team | morning drug |
| Dinger | homerun | hitting head on car door |
| Ducks on the pond | runners on base to be driven in | Boston Common sight |
| Duster | brushback | household tool |
| Eephus pitch | 10-12 feet in air, blooper pitch | no secondary meaning |
| Flake | eccentric player (pitcher) | dandruff |
| Gas | good fastball | result of a Fenway hot-dog |
| Green light | freedom to swing | signals chaos in Boston traffic |
| Hanging curve | curve that doesn't break /easy to hit | your belly after too many beers. |

| Slang | What it Means | Secondary Meaning |
|---|---|---|
| Head-hunting | throwing at batters' heads | the pigeons above |
| Hill | mound | Anita's last name |
| Homer | homerun | Simpsons character |
| Hook | curve | Popular Peter Pan movie |
| Hot corner | 3rd base | street corner in red-light district |
| Long-ball | also a homerun | book by Longfellow |
| Meatball | easy-to-hit pitch | Italian delicacy |
| Mop-up | pitch in relief way behind | janitor's duty |
| No-no | a no-hitter | words used by girlfriend |
| Ohfer | hitless day | grunting noise indicating pain |
| Out pitch | pitch pitcher depends on to get batter out | no secondary meaning |
| Payoff pitch | full count pitch | illegally-funded pitch |
| Punch and Judy hitter | well placed soft singles | puppet who can hit |
| Purpose pitch | pitch thrown at batter to intimidate | politically-correct pitch |
| Quail shot (dying quail) | weak hit dropping in front of outfielders | Murphy Brown's comments |
| Scroogie | screwball pitch | Ebeneezer's nickname |
| Sitting duck | runner is picked off , thrown out easily | ugly duckling's lazy brother |
| Southpaw | left-handed pitcher | left-handed dog |
| Spitball | doctored (Vaseline pitch, pine tar ball) | seen flying off Eifel Tower |
| Stiff | lousy player (used mostly for batters) | your lower back in bleachers |
| Tater | homerun | An American dinner treat |
| Texas league single | lofted weakly into shallow outfield | no secondary meaning |
| Twin killing | double play | bizarre murder case |
| Uncle Charlie | curve ball | your father's brother |
| Wounded duck | weakly hit pop-up | hunter's nightmare |
| Yakker | sharp breaking curve | a good joke |
| Yellow yammer | curve | yellow bird |

# Opposing Managers

**A**s you become a Fenway fanatic you will find yourself disliking the opposing team's manager. Managers come in all different shapes, sizes, and personalities. Here are some basic categories that the other team's manager will likely fall into:

### Ex-Player

- Fiery, wishes he could pick up a bat and take a swing.
- Prone to throwing Gatorade jugs onto the field in anger.
- Often yells at and kicks dirt onto the umpire.

### Gambler

- Manages on gut feeling, "rolls the dice" frequently.
- Goes against conventional wisdom.

### Computer Man

- Too analytical.
- Has all kinds of charts and numbers.

### Text-book Manager

- Too theoretical.
- Manages from the old book.

## Sleeping Beauty

- Sleeps in the dugout, drools.
- Wakes up to call the bull pen, or to make the long walk to the mound (sleep walking?)
- Usually over the age of 55.

## Captain Hook

- Removes starting pitchers too early.
- Shows no patience with his pitchers.

# Dealing with Umpires

*"Many fans look upon an umpire as a necessary evil to the luxury of baseball, like the odor that follows an automobile."* – Christy Mathewson

**Cardinal rule:** Take any call against the Sox as a personal affront to your intelligence and integrity. Your goal is to sway the umpire's allegiance to that of the Red Sox.

## Common Tactics Used with Umpires

- On a call against the home team, yell "Get some glasses!" or "Get your prescription changed!"

- Cheer on the Red Sox manager as he argues with the umpire.

- If the other manager argues, yell, "Kick him out, ump!"

- On close pitches called against the Sox, groan or boo the ump, even if you are 100 feet away in the bleachers.

- If the opposing catcher goes to the mound to confer with his pitcher, groan, boo and yell at the ump to break it up.

# Doing the Fenwave

1. Cheer it on to nurture it at the beginning.

2. Make sure to stand up, throw hands and arms up, and yell loud incoherent things.

3. The wave should only travel from left to right field and around clockwise.

4. Don't start the wave too early in the game — wait until slow moments in the middle innings.

# Special Rules for Dealing with Pitchers

- If the Red Sox relief pitcher is one strike away from ending the game, stand and clap rhythmically with the crowd in anticipation of the last out.

- When a Red Sox relief pitcher comes out of the bull pen to finish the game, bow and pay homage to encourage him if you are in bleachers near the bull pen. You can also yell words of encouragement while he is warming up. For pitchers in the opposing team's bull pen, harass them and try to destroy their confidence. Relief pitchers are usually a wreck mentally because they have to come into pressure-packed situations. They will always pretend they are cool and mean, but inside they're all frazzled.

- If a pitcher has a no-hitter (has not allowed any hits in the game), under no circumstances should you say the words "no-hitter" or directly acknowledge that the pitcher is doing this. It is bad luck, and will surely destroy the pitcher's karma.

CHAPTER FOUR

# POST-GAME TIPS

If you're not too tired after the game and are looking for some fun and food to occupy yourself while traffic dies down, here are some post-game suggestions:

## Souvenirs

### The Souvenir Store — Twins Enterprises
Located on Yawkey Way across from Fenway, this vast souvenir store is the area's best for buying hats, T-shirts, posters, and other sports memorabilia. For small children (and some child-like adults), there is a baseball-shaped cart parked in the middle of the store. (Once upon a time it was used at Fenway to transport pitchers from the bull pen to the mound.) Your child may want to sit in it, and in return you are asked to make a small donation to the Jimmy Fund (Dana Farber Cancer Institute). Among the vast quantities of souvenirs, you will find yourself staring at old, quaint photographs of ballplayers from the past. This store is a must for the serious baseball fan, especially if you want a special souvenir of your Fenway experience.

### The Landsdowne Shop
This souvenir store, located inside Fenway Park, is also accessible from Brookline Ave.

## Bowling/Billiards

### RFA Amusements
(Formerly Kenmore Bowlradome.) Located under Fenway at the corner of Brookline and Landsdowne, this establishment offers 20 lanes of candlepin bowling, video games, and a pool room. Unfortunately, they close early at 10 p.m.

### Jillian's Billiards
Located at the corner of Ipswich and Landsdowne. This establishment contains 40–50 pool tables, a whiffle ball batting cage, a basketball shoot-out game, pinball machines, video games, a table shuffle-board, darts, and foosball, along with two bars and sitting areas. You will not be admitted if you're wearing sweat pants, tank tops, ripped jeans, or hats.

## Night Clubs/Bars

### Avalon, Axis, Bill's Bar and Karma Club
Located along Landsdowne Street, these dance clubs attract patrons clad in dark clothes. If you're wearing chinos with white sneakers, you probably won't be admitted.

### Cask'n Flagon, Boston Beer Works, Linwood Grill
Great for beer or food. The Linwood has live bands on Thursday, Friday, and Saturday nights starting at 10 pm. See chapter 2, pages 48-49 for details.

## Shopping

**Tower Records**

Located on the corner of Newbury St. and Mass. Ave, you'll find three floors of CD's, tapes, and records. With your Red Sox ticket stub you'll receive a $2 discount on most CD's or cassettes over $9.44. This discount also applies at their Cambridge store.

## Leaving

If you're in traffic, turn to WEEI 850 AM for the post-game show starring Joe Castiglione.

Extricating yourself and your car from the surrounding mess is largely dependent on where you parked. If you parked in large, congested lots near Fenway, you will have to endure leaving the lot, traveling along the narrow, winding, one-way streets of Boston, and finally, the traffic on the major highways. If you are one of many New Englanders who suffers from "traffic-phobia," (symptoms include, among other things: mood fluctuations, thrashing, claustrophobia, yelling, displaying profanity, itchiness, sweating), you may want to occupy yourself with some of the surrounding activities for about a half-hour before heading out. If you were smart enough to park away from Fenway, you will enjoy a pleasant walk back to your car, and an easier time leaving Boston.

CHAPTER FIVE

# LIFE BEYOND FENWAY

(YES, IT DOES EXIST)

# Alternatives to the Park: TV and Radio Coverage

When you're not at Fenway you can still follow the Sox on TV for those important 3-game series against arch-rivals. Catch the Sox game either on NESN (New England Sports Network) or on WFXT. Check your local TV listings for the correct station.

Another option is to listen to the game on the radio. There's nothing quite like the experience of imagining the play on the field as the radio announcer paints a picture for you. Moreover, it's great background music that you can listen to while you're doing other stuff. It's tough to remain on the edge of your seat for three hours if you're not at the park. That's why TV or radio work so well while you're doing other things.

Finally, you can find Red Sox information on the internet. Just surf your way to **www.redsox.com.**

# PawSox!

**A**nother great alternative to Fenway is a trip to the Red Sox AAA International Baseball League affiliate, the Pawtucket Red Sox (or PawSox). The PawSox play in Pawtucket, RI, at McCoy Stadium, a small but wonderful place where you will escape all the hustle, bustle, and big-time atmosphere of major league parks. Your seat is always close to the field — capacity is only 7,002. McCoy is a place where kids still seem like the important fans.

McCoy Stadium is famous for the longest game in baseball history, a 33 inning affair which I attended as a youngster in 1981. The PawSox ultimately defeated the Rochester Orioles 3–2. They sell souvenir cups showing the scoring in all 33 innings.

Watching the PawSox at McCoy Stadium is great because it's easy to get there. From Northern points, just follow 95 South into Rhode Island and take exit 2A/Newport Avenue. Following the signs to McCoy, go 2 miles and take a right onto Columbus Ave. The stadium is located on Columbus Ave. If you're coming from the south, take 95N to exit 28/School Street. Bear right at the end of the exit. After two lights, take a left onto Pond Street and you'll spot the stadium.

Ticket prices are cheap — only $6.00 for box seats and $4.00 general admission. Tickets may be purchased in person at McCoy, by mail, or through Ticketmaster. For more information, call the PawSox at (401) 724-7300.

# Following the Sox on the Road

For those of you who do a lot of traveling, you sure know the agonizing feeling of not being able to follow the Sox, especially during a pennant race. Here are some suggestions for keeping up with the team:

1. Read the sports section in *USA Today*. It has the best sports coverage for the traveler, and you can usually find this newspaper anywhere, even overseas.

2. ESPN does good work each night showing highlights of the day's ball games. They also broadcast games several nights during the week. Given the Red Sox's broad appeal throughout the country, you'll probably be able to catch a few Sox games on ESPN no matter where you're traveling.

3. Try going to a baseball game in the city you're visiting. At least you'll be at the park, and all the stadiums show updated scores of all the games around the league so you can monitor the Sox throughout the game. Sampling different parks and stadiums is a lot of fun, and makes you appreciate Fenway's unique qualities.

CHAPTER SIX

# *FANHOOD CHALLENGE*

# Multiple Choice Quiz

**1. Duffy's Cliff was named after:**

    a. Duffy Lewis' beer-belly

    b. 10 ft. high cliff in front of the left field wall

    c. pile of stinky clothes in Duffy Lewis' locker.

    d. cliff in front of dugout

    e. none of the above

**2. If you're planning a last minute trip to Fenway the day of the game, you should first try to:**

    a. buy the tickets just before the game at the ticket office

    b. show up at Gate A and tell security that a Yankee fan stole your tickets

    c. dress up in your Red Sox uniform jersey and go through the players entrance

    d. give up

    e. look for scalpers

**3. If you must buy scalped tickets, you should:**

    a. attach a sign to your chest reading "Need to buy illegal tickets"

    b. ask a police officer where you buy the tickets from scalpers

    c. stand around and look for the slick-looking people murmuring "tickets, tickets.."

    d   turn hat inside-out

    e. none of the above

### 4. One disadvantage of sitting in the bleachers is that:

    a. they're shielded from the sun

    b   you sit on uncomfortable steel benches

    c. you can't walk behind home plate

    d. you can't order beer

    e. none of the above

### 5. Fenway's smallest crowd ever (409) occurred in:

    a. 1928 against the Senators

    b. 1983 against the Indians

    c. 1945 during World War II

    d. 1965 against the Angels

    e. 1978 against the Tigers

### 6. If you're late for the game, your best bet for parking is to:

    a. abandon the car on Landsdowne St., turn your hazard lights on, lift the hood, and run to Gate A

    b. park in the Red Sox parking lot for $10

    c. drive directly into the park and out onto the field (disguise your car as a bull pen cart)

    d. double park on Ipswich Street since they never ticket cars there at night

    e. none of the above will work

7. **The Red Sox will not allow you to bring which of these items:**

    a. can of Sprite

    b. beach ball

    c. inflatable doll

    d. automatic weapon

    e. all of the above

8. **The right field grandstand is less desireable than the left field grandstand because on the right field:**

    a. your neck will hurt

    b. the seats are wooden instead of plastic

    c. you're further from the pizza stand

    d. the sun will be in your eyes

    e. you'll get more foul balls

9. **The real dimensions to the left field wall from home plate are:**

    a. A mystery even to Babe Ruth's ghost

    b. 307 ft

    c. 312 ft

    d. 315 ft

    e. 35 smoots

### 10. Pesky's Pole was named after:

a. Johnny Pesky's favorite pool cue

b. infamous prank by teammates who hung Johnny Pesky's boxer shorts on the flag pole

c. foul pole off which Pesky hit game-winning home run

d. the bat with which Pesky hit three home runs in the 1946 World Series

e. none of the above

### 11. A pitcher throws a 95 mph fastball close to the batter's face. This is called:

a. a scroogie

b. a purpose pitch

c. a dinger

d. an ohfer

e. a spitball

### 12. When a pitcher is pitching a no-hitter, you must:

a. call the local papers at the pay phone behind home plate

b. chant, "no hitter, no hitter!"

c. get on your hands and knees and pray for divine assistance

d. say nothing

e. none of the above

## 13. The Pawtucket Red Sox are famous for:

a. largest attendence ever in minor leagues
b. 33 inning game
c. their spicy clam chowder
d. their incredible cheerleaders
e. ocean view from left field grandstand

## ANSWERS

| | |
|---|---|
| 1. b | 7. e |
| 2. a | 8. a |
| 3. c | 9. c |
| 4. c | 10. c |
| 5. d | 11. b |
| 6. b | 12. d |
| | 13. b |

## SCORING

| | |
|---|---|
| 0–3 correct | Lost Yankee Fan |
| 4–7 correct | "Standing-room-only" peon |
| 8–10 correct | Bleacher bum |
| 11–13 correct | Fenway Connoisseur |

# Fenway Puzzle

Find the 16 hidden words.

```
P  T  L  S  H  S  Q  A  Q  L  O  K  R
E  A  X  W  C  O  O  B  D  T  G  S  K
S  K  Y  B  O  X  R  U  S  P  J  T  B
K  A  W  L  G  P  P  L  X  C  S  R  L
Y  Y  B  E  C  K  F  L  F  I  E  I  E
S  C  R  A  U  B  Z  P  W  T  H  K  J
P  K  L  C  T  O  B  E  S  G  J  E  N
O  J  S  H  E  V  P  N  Y  O  T  A  A
L  N  I  E  W  A  O  K  N  S  O  W  H
E  T  M  R  J  M  G  S  K  I  H  S  P
B  F  I  K  N  O  R  D  U  G  O  U  T
R  C  S  E  C  U  I  I  J  N  M  B  A
U  U  E  G  K  N  C  N  T  S  E  D  T
W  R  K  B  G  D  M  G  H  Z  R  G  E
G  V  L  E  Z  J  L  E  R  A  S  O  R
L  E  R  B  A  B  E  R  U  T  H  B  N
```

Note: Waldo cannot be found in this puzzle.

101

**ANSWER**

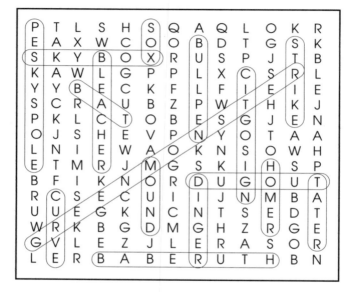

# Fenway in Your Pocket Survey

Please fill out this survey and send it to us now. We appreciate your feedback, and you'll have a chance to **win 4 tickets to a Red Sox game!** We'll also give you official recognition in the book.

Name (optional): _____

Address (optional): _____

_____

_____

Gender: ❑M ❑F

Age range: ❑ under 18  ❑ 18–25  ❑ 26–40  ❑ 40+

What best describes you?

❑ local Red Sox fan

❑ New Englander visiting the Boston area

❑ out of towner visiting the Boston area

❑ other _____

Why did you buy the guide? (Check all that apply.)

❑ souvenir of Fenway

❑ useful info on planning a trip to the park

❑ fun stuff to read about the Red Sox

❑ I didn't buy it, it was given to me as a gift

❑ other _____

How have you been using the guide? (Check all that apply.)

❑ read once for fun and put away

❑ use to plan trips to Fenway

❑ take it with me to the game

❑ other _____

Please share your personal tips and secrets to enjoying a game at Fenway below. If we use your tips we will recognize you in the next edition of this book.

_____
_____
_____
_____
_____
_____
_____
_____
_____
_____
_____

Please let us know if there's any way we can improve this guide. _____

_____
_____
_____
_____
_____
_____
_____
_____
_____

Thanks for your valuable input!

*Mail survey to: Baseball Direct, P.O. Box 6463, Central Falls, RI 02863.*